THE SECRET TO MAKING MORE MONEY IN YOUR JOB IN RETAIL

Easy ways to increase your sales and have fun doing it!

By Erin Lane

Copyright © 2012 Erin Lane
All rights reserved.

ISBN-10:148276914X
ISBN-13:978-1482769142

DEDICATION

This book is dedicated to my children, Tanith and Asher Lane, without whom my life would be pretty pointless and very boring.

ACKNOWLEDGEMENTS

I would like to thank Philip Lane for all the long hours he put into editing. Without you the whole world would know of my aversion to commas.

I would also like to thank Carl Meadows, Adam Lillie, Alex Panayis and Neil Fitzpatrick for their kind words of encouragement and for letting me know that my ideas aren't completely crazy.

I would like to thank all the fantastic people I have worked with over the years who have taught me so much and the companies that have employed me.
Special mention to Lise Williams, a great friend and help in my early days at Myer, Kylie Pitt from Purely Australian whose dedication and energy were inspiring and Alister Norwood for showing me how to be a retailer. Andrew Blanchard, Karen Hammersley, Steve Stone, Linda French, Louise Hanson and Matt Staines from Fantastic Furniture. You guys were the best team I've ever worked with and some of the best friends I ever had and still have. Louise Ward, Jon Harris, Graeme Hosler and Michael Phillington who all helped me to develop my skills as a manager and showed me what commission selling in a hugely competitive environment is all about.

Above all I would like to thank my friends and family who have encouraged me to write this book and who have stuck by me through all my trials and tribulations. Especially my sister Joanne Fitzpatrick, my brother Ryan Greenwell, Julian and Gulianna Angelucci-Deacon, Loz Tweed and Nicola Swadling who have been an enormous support. May all your dreams come true!

CONTENTS

INTRODUCTION 8

Chapter 1: HAVE YOU GOT WHAT IT TAKES? 17

Chapter 2: BACK TO BASICS..................................25

GREETING YOUR CUSTOMER 27

Sell customers on who you are 27

APPROACH 35

Direct Approach 36

Indirect Approach..37

CREATING RAPPORT 41

The trust factor 41

Tips for creating rapport 45

Create rapport and change the world? 47

A warning about jokes 49

QUALIFYING AND QUESTIONING 50

For more sales success, ask the right questions ...50

So what are open questions? 54

SUMMARISING 58

RECOMMENDING 59

PRODUCT KNOWLEDGE..62

Making great features and benefits statements.....65

PRODUCT DEMONSTRATION................................70

TRIAL CLOSES...72

BUYING SIGNALS...74

THE ART OF CLOSING THE SALE 75

Closing questions 77

TURNING OBJECTIONS INTO OPPORTUNITIES 80

How to handle some common objections – What to ask..82

Other methods of overcoming objections :- 83

CUSTOMERS WHO ASK FOR DISCOUNT 87

WARNING ABOUT WHEN THEY WANT TO CHECK WITH SOMEONE ELSE 90

FINISHING THE SALE 93

Add-ons – How to multiply your effectiveness......93

Chapter 3: DEALING WITH CUSTOMER PROBLEMS 102

Chapter 4: ADVANCED SELLING TECHNIQUES......111

It's a numbers game 111

Using social pressure 112

What to say when you get 'Just looking thanks.'.113

Mirroring – How this technique can get the customer to trust you..116

He who speaks first loses – don't try too hard!...118

TROUBLE SHOOTING 121

What was working, isn't working anymore..........121

Your energy level and how they affect your appeal to the customer 123

The importance of consistency in your performance 126

Feedback is a gift (Even if it doesn't feel like it at the time)...128

Perfect practise makes perfect............................130

How never saying 'no' to a customer will get you more sales. 131

How your store is like your toolbox.....................133

Chapter 5: DEVELOPING BEHAVIOURS AND TEAM WORK...135

Sales success begins in your mind......................137

Chapter 6: CHANGING YOUR ORGANISATION FROM WITHIN 140

Chapter 7: SELF ADVANCEMENT 146

Remarkable employees are productive 146

Increasing your corporate profile – how to get ahead 148

Chapter 8: WHAT I LOOK FOR WHEN INTERVIEWING A CANDIDATE 155

How to make the right impression at your interview 155

JUST QUIETLY 159

A word about your appearance 159

Chapter 9: FINAL WORD 161

INTRODUCTION

This book is designed for those of you who have never worked in retail before and would like the low down from a seasoned pro about how it all works so that you can convince a future employer that you can make the change from mechanic or nurse or factory worker, or whatever it is you do now, to a valuable employee in their organisation. In this book is a step-by-step guide to the basics of selling that will get you headed in the right direction for making more money.

It is also designed for those of you who may like to develop better retail skills to be able to go from department store shop assistant to a more challenging and more profitable role in a commission-related environment such as electrical, mobile phones, furniture or real estate.

Commission-based retail jobs can earn you so much more money than regular retail jobs and give you a level of enjoyment that the others just can't. The techniques in this book will take you from being an order-taker to being a top salesperson. It may seem that there is an overwhelming amount of information here and you may think, 'How am I going to do all that in one interaction with a customer?' The answer is that most of this will become automatic after you have been doing it for a while and you won't even know you are doing it. If you start out with the basics before you move onto the advanced techniques you will be just fine. In fact, you will be streets ahead of most of the sales people out there!

There may be some of you who are reading this book that have achieved great success in the above fields of retail and just want a refresher; a get back-to-basics type of journey. There will be many things in here that you already know and hopefully there will also be some you don't, or possibly some things you used to do but have forgotten about. The section on Advanced Selling Techniques will give you hints and tips on how to hone your already considerable skills and increase your income. You want to maximise what you are earning by continuing to increase your skill level. This level is by no means exhaustible, you can get better and better every day and earn more and more money.

The difference between this book and all the others out there is that this book is also about creation. Creating something in your life, your customers' lives and in the culture of the company you work for. It's about you being more than an instrument. It's about you being able to create fulfillment and joy through your job in retail. It's about inspiring those around you and being the best you can be. We have a unique opportunity in retail. We come into contact with hundreds of people every week. If you worked in an office or factory, you would probably only see the same people week in and week out, so being exposed to the public every day is your opportunity to make a difference in people's lives. Large or small differences, it doesn't matter which, the point is to not waste your chance to create a new way of interacting that enhances all our experiences on this planet in our life time. This is the secret to making more money in your job in retail. It's all about what you give to your customer and not what you will get form them. All the great money gurus in the world talk about contribution. What are you contributing to society? How are you enriching their lives?

So, a bit about me and why I am qualified to write a book like this. I have worked in the retail game for the past 27 years, not exactly intentionally, but more because it is something I am just naturally good at. I have purposely increased my skill level over the years by closely observing my colleagues and through all the various training and development courses I have attended, to the point where I can sell anything to anyone as long as I believe in my product and believe it can benefit my customer. I have also developed an ability to put people at ease and make a connection with them. I can make people feel special, respected and valued, which is something everyone wants, but only some have learned the skill of bestowing. It is important that you know that I didn't start off with this skill. I was very shy as a teenager and would avoid interacting with people when I could. This is something I have worked on and continue to do so. Effective communication is the key ingredient in anyone's success and this book will help you to increase your earning potential by making you a better communicator. My purpose in writing this book is to not only give you some very practical and straightforward ideas and techniques to try, but also to share with you how to make the people you meet in your job every day and in your life feel valued and special.

My career started in a department store, where my mother was secretary to the human resources manager. I was to fill in for someone in the stationery department while they worked on the Lego display on the top floor. My natural desire to help people earned me the floor manager's approval and I was offered a Saturday morning job after the Lego display had been packed up. Working at Myer was like working as part of a big family where everyone (well, almost everyone) had the same ideas about how you should treat customers and why we were there. I learned that the customer is always right, never to point, always be polite and to take great care with the customer's purchase. Great foundations to build a service career on. Later I worked for a company that sold souvenir clothing to tourists and it was during my time there that an Australian retail legend by the name of Alister Norwood took over as CEO and it was from him that I learned how to be a retailer. I learned all about attention to detail, driving sales targets, maximising square footage, merchandising and how a retail company should be run. I then went on to work for various fashion retailers, some large, where I learned more, and some small where I was able to put what I had learned from the big guns to good use.

The next step in my journey was at Fantastic Furniture where I sold furniture package deals and it was my first experience of earning commission based on sales over target. It was here that I learned advanced selling techniques from watching my colleagues whose experience was wide and varied. It was here that I also started to earn more money than I ever had before. My income was not limited to what they were willing to pay me. I could earn as much as I wanted to! I watched and learned from Andrew Blanshard who had sold cars and had an amazing ability to read people, an impeccable sense of timing and always knew exactly what to say to his customer. Matt Staines taught me how to create instant rapport with customers and make them feel welcome. You will find more on these guys later. We were a great team and we all taught each other something, often exchanging best practices and talking about how to overcome objections.

A few years later I moved to England and started work as a store manager for T-Mobile. My move to England was a real eye-opener as unlike retail in Australia, sales assistants in England seemed far less willing to help their customers and a much lower standard of work ethic was tolerated. Fast food was slow food, queues were tolerated and cheerfulness was a bit thin on the ground. It was during this time that I began writing this book because it became very clear to me that what I took for granted in the service industry did not appear to be the norm. T-Mobile mind you are a fantastic company whose values are closely aligned to mine which is why I chose to work for them even though I knew very little about technology. They also paid better than most of the other retail companies and with a family to support this was as important to me as I know it is to you.

Chapter 1: HAVE YOU GOT WHAT IT TAKES?

There are many people out there working in factories and warehouses and supermarkets and in petrol stations who are bored with what they do and want a new challenge and may see retail as the next step for them. Some people see it as a glamorous job and if you work in a designer fashion store it may be. What they don't see is the hard work behind the 'glamour.' The endless unpacking of boxes, the constant tidying, the cleaning and general moving about of stock. What they don't see in particular is the courage it takes to approach complete strangers all day every day.

Every human interaction carries with it an element of risk. Every time you speak to another human being on this planet you run the risk of rejection. The secret is that everyone is just as frightened as everyone else out there, so if you feel anxious next time you meet a person for the first time, remember that they are feeling anxious too. What counts is how you deal with the anxiety. It's the thing that makes some people get drunk at parties, it's the thing that makes some people stand behind counters all day. It is the fear of rejection. This is not a good feeling and as salespeople we experience that fear all day every day.

The trick is to ignore that fear and do it anyway. Being a salesperson takes a level of courage and determination that not everyone can muster. If you don't take that risk you will not progress. You will stay in your safe little world, you won't grow or learn and you will remain afraid. I think it helps to know that everyone is just as afraid as you are, no matter how they come across, and if you show courage it gives others the courage to do the same. The more you take that risk, the less risky it will feel over time and the easier it will become. You may get some rejections, but you will get more acceptances if you practice your rapport-building skills. There is lots of advice on creating rapport in this book. I don't get rejected very often anymore, as my greetings are now so warm and so welcoming that my customers want to respond. They want more of what I am offering them in just one sentence. They feel like I am their friend. People without courage will avoid the human exchange and consequently will fail to develop the skills to interact socially in a comfortable way. Those of us who have the courage will feel the fear and choose to interact despite it. Gradually, over time, the fear becomes less and less and you will find yourself able to interact quite comfortably in most situations. Don't kid yourself though, the fear never goes away completely! All those people out there who you think are sublimely comfortable and cool and so sure of themselves, still have that small fear inside them of the unknown and are therefore just as vulnerable as the rest of us.

So what is it about salespeople that are different from your average Joe? They have chosen to step up to the mark each day and overcome their fears and connect with people. It takes courage to do this and conviction to do it every day. You need to ask yourself if you are ready to take this on. Do you have what it takes to keep going if you are rejected or ignored when you approach someone? How will you process this feeling? Will you drift closer to the counter and end up behind it where you know that people want you to talk to them? Will you feel insulted? Will you get angry and be rude? Will you just stop approaching people? How you deal with this is up to you. I find a silly saying works for me. When I say hi to someone and they ignore me I say, 'Have a banana Erin' and have a little laugh to myself. All that has happened is the person you have said hello to either did not heard you or is trying to avoid interaction with you, the stranger, out of their own fears. Some people believe that a salesperson is 'out to get them', take them for a ride or rip them off. I once said hi to someone, they ignored me, I said my little saying and it turned out they were deaf. I'd said hi from behind them and they didn't even know I'd spoken! It is your job, and mine, to show people that we are there for them and because of them, that we have their best interests at heart and are at their service.

Your may find yourself, after reading this, more aware of your fears when you approach people but that is a good thing because becoming aware of something is the first step to mastering it.

So the message here is push on through the fear and the rejection to the good stuff, which is rapport, fun, achievement and financial reward.

Another thing that a great salesperson has is an unshakable belief that they will hit their targets and make the sale every day with every single customer. They know they are great sales people and that their customer is in good hands. They have practised their skills and continue practising every day. They know how to think positively and to turn their failures or short-comings into an opportunity to grow and learn. If you have the capacity to tell yourself every day that you are a fantastic sales person and to really believe it, the money will come.

Ultimately it comes down to passion. Have you got a passion for people? Does it give you a good feeling when you have helped someone? Brightened their day? You need to care about people. No matter who they are. Some people you will like, in fact, most people you will like if you work at it. Some people you won't, but the better you get at interacting with your fellow human beings the better life will be for you. How fantastic is it that we retailers get to spend each day with a vast array of people? So many of us with so many opportunities to create a great place to live in. Imagine if you could spend all day every day being kind to someone? Imagine if you could help these people all day long. Imagine if you could turn a community around by being kind and courteous, and polite and helpful and caring? Really caring about the people you come into contact with each day. Making them feel special and cared for. Really understand them. Isn't it just the best feeling when you feel understood?

Listen. Every religion in the world advocates being kind to others. Give to your community. Listen. Every person you meet in your life can teach you something if you just listen to them. Ask them questions about themselves. People tell me all sorts of things about their lives. Countries they have visited, or lived in, diseases they have had, famous people they have met, jobs they have worked in, all sorts of stories. There is such a rich tapestry of experience and knowledge out there in the public realm that you have the opportunity to tap into. You just have to be bold enough to ask the questions and then listen to what people have to say. Everyone you meet in your life can teach you something. Some people believe that everyone we meet is 'sent' to us so that we can learn. Okay, so some people will teach you how to bite your tongue and keep your cool. Others will wake you up a little bit and make you realise just how lucky you are. Some people will give you information about the weather. So what I am saying here is go into each interaction with an enquiring mind and you will always get something back. Did I mention you need to listen?

Chapter 2: BACK TO BASICS

Every company I have worked for in my long career in sales has a different system of selling and a different number of steps. Guess what? They all worked. The reason they all worked is because they all had the most effective things in common. One guy I worked for had three simple ones. Rapport. Suggest. Persist. Easy right? Well, it is if you understand how to do all three. I worked for another company that had six. One company had five, but had two or three subsections to each step. The thing is, you can call it what you like, a process, a plan, steps, whatever and you can have as many or as few as you like and call them whatever you want. The company you work for has its methods and will want you to follow those methods, so do it.

They will work. What you will find in this chapter is a full explanation of the steps that most companies use although they may call them different things. I will also explain why we use the different steps and how important it is that you don't miss any. If you find anything in here that your company does not do, then it is only going to benefit you in the long run anyway, so you may as well try a few. Everyone has their own style and the more of your own self, your own personality, you can bring into your interaction with your customers the better.

So here are the basics in black and white. Follow them and you will be guaranteed more success and a larger income.

GREETING YOUR CUSTOMER

Sell customers on who you are

As someone once said, 'You only get one chance to make a good first impression...' (I know it's an awful cliche but like so many cliches it's true) so your greeting is vital. Please note here that a greeting is very different to approaching someone to offer service. Read that again. It is not going up to someone and saying, "Can I help you?" A greeting is the thing you do to welcome the customer to the store and let them know, that you know they are there. If you get this wrong, you may be finished before you've begun.

Generally speaking, you will have no more than 30 seconds to do this before the customer will assume that they will not get any service in this store and they may leave. They may leave with the impression that you are unwilling, rude, uncaring, unprofessional or hopeless at your job, so make sure you get the greeting across because we both know that you are none of those things. Would you stay somewhere where you thought you would be given attention, but were ignored? The customer must be given a greeting or at least acknowledged within that 30 second window of opportunity. It may not seem very long to you, but stop reading now and get yourself a watch or clock with a second hand and walk around as if you are in a shop for 30 seconds and you will realise that it is quite a while.

The other thing you need to consider is how early is too early to greet your customer. This will depend on the type of store and the greeting you give. Have you ever been into a store and had someone pounce on you immediately and a bit too enthusiastically within seconds of your foot crossing the threshold? Yikes! It's bloody awful! Do not do this. Work out where in the store it is acceptable for the customer to get their first bit of interaction from you. I did this recently with a store team and we worked out where the 'green zones' (where it is safe to speak to the customer) and the 'red zones' (where it is too early to speak to the customer) were, by pretending to be customers entering the store. The red zone was from the doorstep to about two meters in (it was a very big barn of a store). The green zone was the rest of the store. Mind you, we did find that if you were being greeted on your way out of the store, that didn't really work either. So remember, don't pounce and don't leave it too long. Experiment a little and you will find the perfect place. If you find this sweet spot, spend as much time in it as you can. The more customers you greet, the more sales you will make. It will pay off as money in your pocket.

So what makes a good greeting and what makes a spectacular greeting?

Let me tell you about Matt Stains. Matt was a guy I worked with in a furniture store. He was about 30, had funny hair and the best smile you've ever seen. Matt's way of greeting people was also the best I've ever seen. He said that he imagines that he is holding a party in the store and the people who walk in are friends of friends that he hasn't met yet, but would like to get to know. Brilliant! How would you greet people if it was your party and you were the gracious host? I have used this since being given this gift by Matt and it never fails. Sometimes I greet people this way and they look kind of curious, as if they can't quite work out if they already know me or not, or where they have met me before. If you can master this technique, your intention will come across in your greeting and it will make the person feel comfortable and welcome. This is your main goal at this point. Make them feel comfortable and welcome.

But, lets get down to the basics.

First eye contact has to be established and it must be accompanied by a smile. The smile must be warm, open and engaging. Please don't go over the top with the smile. If you are grinning like a loony you will just frighten people off and make small children cry. It needs to be the type of smile you would give to someone you already know and haven't seen for a while.

What you say to a customer is up to you and how you use your personality, but there are a few rules to follow:

1. It should be sincere

2. It should be professional in that you shouldn't use slang or colloquialisms

3. You should feel comfortable saying it

4. You should vary it throughout the day and from customer to customer especially if it is busy so you don't sound like a robot

5. If you are busy with someone else you must always give eye contact and nod or smile. If you can, let them know how long you will be with the other customer. I have seen customers wait to see a salesperson for over 30 minutes because they were given a warm greeting and a few smiles.

6. The 3 meter rule – if you come within 3 meters of a customer in your store, even if they are being served by someone else, you must give them an acknowledgement, a nod, smile or greeting.

Everyone is different and has their own style, but here are the types of things you might greet a customer with are:-

Hi

Hi there

Lovely weather we are having

Hello

Good morning or afternoon

How are you today?

Not rocket-science is it?

So you have made eye contact and delivered your greeting and the customer says, 'just looking thanks' and dismisses you. Why do they do that? Mainly it's an automatic response to the usual question they get when a salesperson speaks to them. Most salespeople will ask, "Can I help you?" Even if you haven't said,"Can I help you?" people will automatically respond with "Just looking thanks". Never, never, never, never say, "Can I help you?" unless you are offering help, such as when someone is struggling with something like changing a tyre. Just greet them! The only exception is if you are at the counter and have just finished serving someone and the next person steps up, you can do both in quick succession – "Hi!" (greeting) "What can I do for you today?" (offer of service).

There is more about how to handle, 'I'm just looking' in the chapter on Advanced Selling Techniques.

Your body language should be open at this stage of the process. What do I mean by that? You should be facing your customer with a relaxed stance, arms by your sides. What is closed body language? Arms folded, being side on or back turned, hands behind your back, slouching on the counter, hands in pockets or any other posture that signifies that you aren't really interested in serving them.

Just another note on greeting the customer. Customers who are acknowledged in stores and spoken to by sales people are far less likely to shoplift than those who are left alone, so a good way to reduce your store's shrinkage is to increase your greeting and acknowledging.

APPROACH

After you have greeted the customer and given them a little space to relax and look around your store you need to approach them with an offer of service. This should generally happen well within 3 minutes, but check with your employer how long they would like you to take between the two steps.

If your customer is feeling comfortable and relaxed it will be easy to approach them and offer service. This is the point I talked about earlier where you must overcome your fear of rejection and begin creating rapport with your customer.

You must continue to smile and you can use a direct or indirect approach. The best approach is one that builds rapport with the customer which is an indirect approach, as this will help build a relationship that could have them come back to you time and time again. However, sometimes customers are in a hurry and you can tell by their body language that they are on a mission and need to get things done quickly in which case the direct approach is best. What does this body language look like? Hurried steps, quickly glancing around to spot what they are after, making eye contact with you and moving toward you, checking their watch or a worried expression.

Direct Approach

This approach is where you immediately offer assistance to the customer.

Examples are:-

What can I do for you today?

What brings you into the store today?

You look like you are on a mission, what are you after?

What are you looking for? (after 'just looking thanks')

You look like you are in a hurry, what can I do for you?

Indirect Approach

This approach is focussed on creating rapport with the customer and putting them at ease. It is preferable to the direct approach as you will be better able to start a relationship with the customer that is ongoing and will get you repeat business and will lead to the customer recommending you and your service to all their friends and family. These sorts of questions are designed to get the other person talking, to give you some information about them and to show them that you find them interesting and that you know how to listen. You must give them your full attention at this stage.

You must be present. What do I mean by being present? Being present with someone means every fibre of your being is focused on them and your interaction with them. You are not thinking about what you will have for lunch or how the electricity bill is overdue or that you need more teabags. You are there with them and only them for that exact moment. You will be amazed by the effect this has on people. Go and practice it right now with someone, anyone near you. Be there for them. Ask them about themselves and really listen to what they have to say. This will let your customer know that you care about them and what they are trying to achieve. It will make them feel special also, and isn't that what every single person on the planet wants? To feel special. To feel important and that they count in the grand scheme of things? It is your job as an employee to make them feel this way and it is your mission in life as a human being to make other people feel this way also. What will you get out of it? Plenty. How will it make you feel? Fantastic! Right there and right then, they are the most important person in the world.

Some examples of an indirect approach to get you started are:-

If they have children with them that are running amok, ' kids driving you mad are they?'

If they have shopping bags, 'looks like you've been busy'

'I like your shoes/bag/top/ring/necklace' etc.

Speaking to the children or commenting on how cute they are

Talking about the weather (a great one for countries like England where people are a bit reserved or for when you sense the customer is a bit shy of interacting with you)

Talking about how busy/quiet the shopping centre is

Ask about what they are wearing, for example – 'I see you are wearing an 'I love Canada' t-shirt. Did you go there, or did some other lucky person bring it back for you?'

So what have you been doing/been up to today?

You will find your own style in this regard and indeed some of the above may sound completely wrong to you. The general idea is that you **do not talk about the product directly or immediately.**

CREATING RAPPORT

The trust factor

If you want to enjoy your job, make your customer happy and get them to come back time and again and tell their friends about what great service they got, you have to create instant rapport. It may take years of practice or you may have a natural talent for it but it is all about connecting with the customer in a way that makes them feel understood, relaxed and in safe hands. You need to have confidence in yourself to do this effectively. If you feel relaxed and are enjoying the experience of meeting them, it will give them license to feel the same way.

People do not buy products until they have bought you. If they trust you and believe that you have their best interests at heart they will buy what you suggest, confident in the knowledge that the product is the right one for them.

Some of the most charismatic people in the world, movie stars, world leaders and people who run large corporations, have one thing in common, they know how to make the people they are interacting with feel special. Your objective here is to give the customer, your new best friend, your complete and undivided attention. Like I said before, be present with them. Bring your whole self into their world. When they are speaking, look directly at them and lean forward slightly. Imagine they are telling you the secret of life, the universe and everything. Imagine that they are the most interesting person you have ever met and what they are telling you is greatest pearl of wisdom you have ever heard. You will be amazed by the effect this has on people. Another point to make here is, why shouldn't you give this person your undivided attention? Surely we are all worthy of this level of respect, care and understanding. I'm sure you would expect if from someone you were doing business with, so of course you must give them this gift. After all, you will be taking their money which earns you money, so it is the least you can do. The better you get at doing this, the more money you will make. You get nothing without giving first.

So how do you get someone you have never met before and have only known for a few minutes to trust you? This is where your true intention of being in the role you are in comes in to play. If you truly want to help people, if you truly care about how people perceive your company, if you truly care about people in general, you will have no trouble with this. It will come across in everything you say, in your body language, people will see it in your eyes and feel it instinctively about you. If you don't feel this way about people, you are in the wrong profession. Get out! You give good salespeople a bad name.

Okay, so we all have days when we can't quite muster feelings of love and devotion to the human race, so what do you do on those days? You need to 'fake it, till you make it'. I know that kind of goes against what I am saying in this chapter, but I am also talking about you and you are a human being! You will have times in your life when it gets tough to stay positive. You know, the dog is sick, you have too many bills and not enough money, you had a row with your partner, the car breaks down. It can all get a bit much sometimes. Here's a secret for you. Your brain releases a chemical called endorphins. Endorphins are released when you exercise, when you eat chocolate and when you have sex. They also get released when you smile. The muscles in your face make your brain release this chemical which goes to the receptor sites in your brain for endorphins and you get a happy feeling. That's why you feel great after a good laugh. The muscles in your face are doing their thing and releasing those chemicals in the brain. So if you 'fake it' by acting happy or jolly and smiling a lot, then you will start to feel better. Pretty soon all those negative feelings will float away and you won't be faking anymore. If you ever saw me driving to work some days, you might be a bit alarmed at the strange faces I was pulling to get that endorphin hit. You may have seen those classes you can go to, where people stand about and practise their laughing. This is the same principle.

I have to tell you, throughout my life I have had the usual ups and owns and some of my downs have been doozies! I feel so grateful that I have worked in an environment where I have been able to forget all those troubles and just focus on making my customer happy. It's such a relief from feeling worried, upset, down and just plain awful. For eight hours I was able to forget all that and just focus on other people. Focusing on others can only benefit you. Give to people- it's what we are here for. If you look after your customers they will become repeat customers and the money will come, so you don't have to do the job only for love or the health of the planet.

Tips for creating rapport

Ask questions!

People love to talk about themselves and what they are doing. They will think that you are great if you listen to them intently. To do this you have to maintain good eye contact, concentrate on what they are saying, comment on what they are saying from time to time and don't allow yourself to be distracted by what is going on around you. You really have to get into their world. Be present. Give them your complete and undivided attention and make them feel as though what is happening for them in that moment is just as important to you as it is to them. Connect with them on a human to human level, without judging them, without having an internal dialogue commenting on what they are saying. Just really listening will make them feel as though you really get what they are saying. This is the greatest gift you can give to someone and they will remember you for it. They may not be able to articulate what it is about you that they liked but they will know that they liked being around you. People may not always remember what you say, but they will remember how you made them feel. They will feel cared for.

You can project this within seconds after a bit of practice and your customer will instantly feel at ease and know they are in good hands. You will feel like their friend. You have recognised in each other the humanity we all have in common. Be there for them and get into their world.

Create rapport and change the world?

The other thing I want to discuss is the unique opportunity we all have of influencing the general happiness and mental well-being of the planet. What are you saying? How can I influence the general happiness and mental well-being of the planet? It sounds a bit crazy, right? Hear me out. Okay, let's say you are a salesperson in a store and you come into contact with 20 people a day. Let's say you work with 10 other people who also come into contact with 20 people each a day. So as a team in your store you have influence over the general happiness and mental well-being of 220 people. If those 220 people have a great time in your store and leave feeling happy and satisfied, knowing that good service is not dead and that there are kind, interested, polite and caring people in the world after all, you have influenced their mental well-being and happiness. If those 220 people go home in a good mood and are kind and loving to their partner and 1.8 children that is about 660 more people who may find their days or even lives slightly brighter because of you. In just one day. Over a year that's about 15,000 people. Now imagine that 100,000 people read this book and make their customers days brighter. Suddenly there are a whole lot of people caring for the general happiness and mental-wellbeing of the planet. Say this book is read by 100,000 people in each country in the world and they all make someone's day brighter. What a world we would live in! It doesn't cost you anything. In fact, it pays to approach your work this way. You get personal satisfaction, you will have people you come into contact with leaving you feeling enriched from the experience, you get financial reward, recognition from your peers and your boss and you get a better world to live in. You are there for the 8 hours a day, so why not? Why not get as much out of each working day as you can? Why wait for the weekends or your days off to enjoy yourself? It's up to you.

A warning about jokes

Be very careful about joking with your customer. You have to be very good at gauging a person's sense of humor before you attempt this tricky rapport-building approach. It can backfire massively and if you attempt it and it doesn't work, there really is no going back. I once joked with a customer, who had bought a phone on which the backlight didn't stay on long enough for her to read her emails, that she would just have to read really fast (said with a smile) before I solved her problem. It turned out she was dyslexic. So, not so funny after all. I'm not saying not to have a laugh with people, just that it may be better to wait for them to crack a joke and join in with them.

QUALIFYING AND QUESTIONING

For more sales success, ask the right questions

Questioning your customer is the most important thing to do correctly. You may be able to get away with a less than fantastic greeting, but get this bit wrong and you will go nowhere and earn no money. So pay attention! Your obligation as a salesperson is a moral one. You have to believe that you are not only providing a service in helping a customer choose a product, but to be successful you must help the customer to choose the correct product according to the information they give you. It is not up to you to decide for the customer what is right for them. It is your duty to help them uncover their needs. Salespeople who don't do this, who sell what will get them a bigger commission or more prestige in their company or whatever it is they get, give salespeople a bad name. They are not interested in doing the right thing by their customer, or even by their company, only themselves. Okay, so you might be thinking that the company wants you to make as many sales as you can. That is true, but most companies don't look at their customers as a one-off sale. They work out how much each customer might spend with them over their lifespan. They talk about customer advocacy - customers telling their friends and family about your company and how great it is. So yes, the company wants you to make sales, but they want quality as well as quantity. The customer experience needs to be great in order for them to continue to shop with you. It is vital that you meet the customer's needs fully while balancing that with what your company asks of you.

So what does qualifying mean and why do we do it? Well it's not asking the customer to fill in a form to see if they are good enough for you to spend time with, but it is important that you know one thing. ARE THEY BUYING TODAY? This question is very important in some stores and not so important in others, but it is a good idea to find out either way. Why? Because you need to know how much time to spend with the customer. There is no use spending an hour with someone who is not ready to buy. Imagine you greet the customer, start building rapport, question them, find out what they want, spend time explaining the product to them, discuss prices, and they agree that this is the product they want. Then they say, "oh, but I'm not buying today...." Goodness me! What a complete waste of time! If you had known at the beginning that they were only gathering information and ideas about what to get, but were unable or unwilling to purchase there and then, you would have been much better off just building some rapport (so they will come back to you), giving them a bit of information and telling them how you will help them get what they need when the time is right. The feeling you get when you make this mistake is so disheartening that you will learn very quickly how not to make it. If you work in a busy environment you will need to do this all day long. When I worked as a Store Manager for T-Mobile I would spend all day Saturday qualifying people. I would find out what they needed and did they want it today, then queue them up for sales people to do their thing and sell them the product. Trust me, you will save yourself a lot of heartache and time if you remember to find out if they are ready to purchase before you begin your fantastic sales pitch.

So how do we get the information needed in order for the customer to make an informed decision and for us to show them the correct items? Open questions! Lots and lots and lots of questions. I have interviewed people for jobs in the past and one of the things I got them to do in the interview was to sell a holiday. Some of them were great and asked me lots of questions about what I wanted, who was going with me, what sort of climate I was looking for, when I wanted to go etc, while others just read through the info pack they were given and then asked me which one I wanted. We can all do that for ourselves. I can look up info on the internet and read everything and make a decision. Easy. What I can't do is narrow it down quickly to just a few choices that suit me perfectly. That is your aim. To save the customer time and money by finding the right product for them. Effective questioning will get you to that point. What type of questions you will ask depends on your product but the general idea is to reduce the number of choices from your entire store to just a few items. If you don't do this you will end up doing a show and tell tour of all the items in the store. It would be like going up to each item and asking. 'Do you like this? Do you like this? What about this?' Totally tedious and not something that impresses a customer. It wastes everyone's time. You might think that this is a silly example, but I've seen it done!

So what are open questions?

Open questions begin with:

Who – who is the product for? Who will be using it?

What – what types of functions does it need to have? What do they need it to do? What colour are they looking for? What size do they need?

When – when will the product be used or when do they need it by?

Where - where will the product be used? Where will they store it?

How – how much do they want to spend? How long does it need to last? How are they going to use it?

Why – why are they looking for the product? Why are they looking for this product in particular and not something else similar? Be careful not to sound like you are interrogating them on this one, gently gently.

Which – which colour do they prefer

And tell me about ….. Which is a great way of asking why gently, as in, so tell me about how you use your computer.

You will need to ask enough of these questions to narrow down the range of products you have to the ones most suitable to them. Ultimately you want 2 or 3 products for them to choose from. Any more than this and you will be in danger of giving them too much to choose from and therefore make it difficult for your customer to say yes to one product and buy it.

You are also trying to find out what the motivation is for them to buy the product. Once you have their motivation you can cater to their needs quite easily, without running the risk of offering the wrong product. This will become very important when you are closing the sale so ask yourself these questions as you go along. The customer will give you the clues to the answers, you just need to read between the lines a little.

What is it they need the product to do?

What functions does it need to perform?

How do they want it to make them feel?

How will it improve their quality of life?

Is it a luxury item?

Is this a reward they are giving themselves or someone else?

Will it make them feel safe?

Will it make them feel successful?

Will it make them feel proud?

Is how their ownership of the product perceived by others important to them?

Does it need to impress people?

Do they want it to be unobtrusively impressive?

Are they more interested in the value they are getting or the product they are buying?

If you haven't narrowed the choice down to 2 or 3 items, you need to go back and question some more until you do.

SUMMARISING

When you have finished your questions, you need to repeat back to the customer in summary form, what they have just told you. Eg, " So you are after a 2-seater lounge-suite with a high back, padded arms in a corded fabric, in blue, with fabric protection so the kids don't mess it up. And you need it delivered by the end of the week. It that right?' Summarising is so important. It lets the customer know you have heard them, it lets you know that you have understood your customers needs correctly, and if you done it right, closing the sale will be easy because you have met their needs. If the customer has given you all the information, you have narrowed down the range and they have agreed that the product is suitable, why wouldn't they say yes to taking it?

RECOMMENDING

Once you have narrowed down your range to 2 or 3 that suit the customer's needs, you need to make a recommendation. This is, what you recommend given the information you have received from the customer. If you haven't listened carefully and summarised back to the customer what they need, you will know immediately because they will not accept your recommendation. If you find that your customer is rejecting everything that you are showing them, there are only 2 proper reasons for it. Either you have missed something or misunderstood something in your questioning to do with their needs, or you have their motivation wrong. If this happens, you will need to go back to questioning them before you go any further in your recommendations. If you don't the customer will just walk out thinking you are an idiot because you didn't understand what they were after.

If you have got it right, however, and have created good rapport, the customer will usually listen to what you suggest because they trust you and because you have taken the time to find out the right information. You need to know your products at this stage too narrow down the possibilities. As you become more experienced in your field you will know which questions you have to ask first. For example, when I worked in a furniture store, the first question I always asked after discovering that the customer was looking for a new sofa was, 'When do you need it by?' If they needed it immediately, this narrowed down our range to what we had in stock in the warehouse. I would then ask what sort of configuration they wanted - 2- and 3-seater, modular etc which narrowed it down further, and then colour choice, until I was left with perhaps 2 or 3 items out of a possible 1000 variations on 'a new sofa'. The same goes for clothing: there are thousands of items in a store. First question answered might be 'jeans'. Next would be colour, then style, then size. Electronics, a TV, size, functions required, in stock or ordered etc. You get the drift?

So you have narrowed down your product range, now you can begin to actually sell the item/s to them. Note here that until now the only thing you have sold to the customer is yourself and if you have done this well, the rest is easy.

If you are starting a new job, ask your colleagues or listen to them selling to find out the questions you need to ask to narrow down the range. Chances are if they have been there a long time, they will know exactly which questions to ask.

PRODUCT KNOWLEDGE

I can't stress enough how important it is that you know everything you can about the product you are selling.

Product knowledge should be provided to you by your employer, but if you don't know enough or want to know more, ask! The more you know the more value the customer will see in the item. You will also sound more confident and reliable if you are able to rattle off the features and benefits of the product than if you are scrabbling around for information or umming and ahhing about what it can or can't do. If you wanted to sell someone a Bentley you would need to know more than that it is blue, has four doors, leather seats and goes well. So do your homework.

It is also important that you know the approximate if not the exact price of the items in your store so that you can direct the customer to right product within their budget range. For example, if a customer wanted to revamp their spare bedroom cheaply, you wouldn't show them a bedroom-suite that costs thousands.

The other thing you need to know about your product is - do you have it in stock? There is nothing worse than spending time with a customer selling them something they can't have until a later date when they want it right there and then. You need to SELL THEM WHAT YOU'VE GOT. Most people I have worked with have at some point complained that the store doesn't have such and such. They sometimes even justify their poor performance this way. I'm not saying that the lack of a popular item will not affect the overall volume of what you sell because it will. What I am saying is if you don't have an item in stock, first don't sell that item and second, if the customer really wants that item, find out why. They may be just as happy with something else that is similar and will do the job equally as well. If you find out their needs through open questions you may find that they don't really need the popular item, which is usually more expensive due to the advertising costs that made it so popular. You may even be able to save the customer some money. For example, at T-Mobile, for a long time we didn't sell the iPhone. People would walk through the door all day long asking if we had it. These people were looking for something we didn't sell, but why did they want it? What was it about the iPhone that they wanted so much? I asked them, what was it they wanted the phone to do? Were they aware of how expensive it was? I then told them about what we sold that had similar functions and compared what they would pay for the iPhone to what they would pay for our similar item. Sure it didn't always work, some people just wanted the iPhone because it was an iPhone because it was an iPhone and because it was an iPhone. It was more of a fashion statement to them than a useful tool to access the internet on, but some of those customers did take our similar product. If I had never asked them why they wanted an iPhone I would have missed out on those sales. I knew my products and what they could do for the customer. SELL WHAT YOU'VE GOT!

Making great features and benefits statements

At this stage, your rapport building will really show its true value. If you have built good rapport, you will know little things about the customer that will give you clues to what your customer's like and dislikes are. If you use the information they have given you at the rapport stage, you will be even better able to say the things that show your customer that you have listened and that you care. Okay, so that's a bit vague isn't it? Here's an example. Remember the guy in the I Love Canada T-shirt? Let's say I've asked him if he's been there? If he says, "No, I could never afford that", you would know that he may not want to pay top dollar and needs good value for money. If he said, "Yes, I go there twice a year for a holiday to visit my family", you may be able to suggest a delivery service for gift giving. If you were selling furniture you might enquire if they visit him and he needs a spare bed or foldout sofa. If you are selling mobile phones, you might suggest an international calling package. You get the idea? Every piece of information you get in the rapport-building stage can have an influence over what you show them and how you sell them what you have. The customer knows you have listened and that you care because you are suggesting something based on what they have already told you.

You may have heard of features and benefits before and indeed explain them quite well to your customers, but first let's examine why you would tell the customer about the features of a product. Apart from the obvious need for the customer to know what they are buying and that the product is right for them, the other reason we explain the features and benefits is to **increase the value of the product in the customer's eyes.** The more you can tell the customer about a product and how it will benefit them, the more value the product takes on. For example if I say, ' this dining-table comes with wooden chairs' you might think, 'good, I like wood'. If however, I say, "this dining table comes with 6 beautiful mahogany chairs, with padded seats for extra comfort, and a shaped back. So, you can sit on one of theses after the meal at your dinner party without feeling as though you have to get up immediately because the chair is digging into your back. Also where the seat meets the back there are 9 fixing points for added strength and durability, so these chairs will last you a long time." Can you appreciate how differently the customer will now view the product? One is a wooden chair, the other is a wooden chair that is also comfortable and will last them a long time. Which would you rather buy and which one would you pay more to have? In fact, if your customer is objecting to the price of the product, it is a good idea to go over the features and benefits again to show the customer the value of the product. In the case of Mr 'I love Canada' who could never afford to go there, durability is probably very important.

So what is a feature?

A feature is a physical attribute of the product, e.g. it is made of wood, silk, glass, plastic. It has buttons, a zip, is oval, is 5cm long, is made in England, is Gucci. It is something that describes the product in some way.

A benefit is something about the feature of the product you are describing that will benefit the customer and suit their needs.

For example, it is made of wood, so it will be long-lasting. It is made by Gucci so it is of good quality, will last and will be an impressive/stylish piece to own. It is made of glass so it will let light through.

A feature and benefit statement is a sentence you make up to explain to the customer why you are suggesting this item to them. You will need to know these statements off by heart and you can practice them with your colleagues. The more you tell a customer about the product the easier it will be to sell it.

It is important to note that you must give the customer information in small chunks, allow them to digest the information and **avoid jargon** at all costs. Using industry jargon will confuse your customer and make them feel stupid. For example, " This phone had GPRS, HSDPA, an MP3, 3G, quadband, 16MB and a 5 mp camera." What? Some people may know what I'm talking about, but your granny probably doesn't. The amount of information a customer needs varies, so by giving it to them in small chunks and in plain language you will be better able to gauge when to stop giving them the information and move on to asking for the sale. I once bought a microwave from a guy who rabbited on for 5 minutes about all the amps and watts and things the microwave had, but all I wanted was something that would look good in my kitchen. He could have just asked me what the most important thing was that I wanted it to have and saved himself a lot of time and energy. He didn't ask me what I was looking for the product to do, if I remember correctly he didn't ask me anything at all! He simply went down the show and tell route of describing each item. This had the effect of making him seem very knowledgable, which was great, but he wasted my time. Questioning is key.

PRODUCT DEMONSTRATION

It is very important, when showing a customer a product, that you get them to handle it, sit on it, try out the functions on it or touch it in some way. By this I don't mean you show them how, I mean you get them to do it. If I was selling a vacuum cleaner and wanted to demonstrate how much stuff it can suck up, I could do what most people do and throw the dirt on the carpet and then suck it up with the fantastic product, or I could give them the vacuum and ask them to clean the carpet. Which do you think would be more effective? The answer is of course, getting them to use the product! This has the effect of the customer beginning to feel ownership of the product. Get it into their hands! If the customer likes what you are showing them, they will be reluctant to hand it back to you, or if they don't like it they will give it back to you and you will know they don't want it and you can show them something else. If the customer doesn't like it, don't ever think that the sale is over. Show them something else! Keep going until they buy or all possibilities are exhausted.

One word of advice here, make sure if you demonstrate a product, that you know what you are doing and that it is in perfect working order. It puts people off if you are fiddling about trying to get something to work or randomly pushing buttons in the hope that it will do something to impress the customer. This type of demonstration will make the customer lose faith in you, in what you are telling them, and makes the product look difficult to use.

TRIAL CLOSES

Trial closes are questions you ask the customer in the process of selling the item. When you are talking about a product to the customer you need to ask them questions. You need to ensure that you are on the right track with what you are suggesting they purchase. If you can get your customer to admit that the product fulfills their needs several times during the sale, asking the final closing question will be much easier. Also if they say yes, yes, yes to all your trial closes they are going to feel a bit silly saying no to the closing question. It is not your intention, however, to make them feel silly, it's just how people feel naturally if they agree all along and then don't agree at the end. So by asking trial closing questions they are more likely to say yes to your closing question.

- Is that the sort of colour you are looking for?
- Does that sound like what you are after?
- What do you think so far?
- Will that do the job do you think?

At this stage the customer will either say, yes, that is what I'm after or no, it's not. Either way you have somewhere to go. If they don't like it, this will help you to find out what it is about the product they don't like and you will be better able to direct them to a product that suits them better. If they do like it, you know you are on the right track and can keep going towards asking for the sale. Without this technique, you could end up trying to sell the customer something they don't want or like for some reason and they will not buy. Some people will not tell you directly that they don't like what you are showing them because they are worried that they will insult you or your product. Listen for weak responses or reluctant agreement such as "yeah it's not bad" or "mmm it's alright". It is important to read their body language here. If they are not looking at you, smiling or nodding, they probably don't want the item.

BUYING SIGNALS

Nodding along with what you are saying

Rubbing the chin with their fingeritps

Fiddling with a necklace or chain

Handling the item and asking questions about it

Spending time looking at the item

They seem excited and are smiling lots

So here you are. You've created the rapport, you've found out what the customer needs, you've suggested exactly what the customer is looking for and they like what you have shown them. Now what?

THE ART OF CLOSING THE SALE

The biggest mistake salespeople make is to go through the entire process with their customer, create the rapport, ask all the right questions, explain the product and then not ask for the sale! YOU HAVE TO ASK FOR THE SALE. Otherwise you have wasted your time and you have also wasted the customer's time. The great Michael Maratheftis said, "The customer is King!". He also said, "Get their money!" It's a matter of balancing the two.

Think about it. Your company pays you good money to be on the shop floor and to spend time talking to customers. The customer has bothered to get out of bed, get dressed, get in the car/on the bus or train, organised their entire day around coming into your store and all you give them is information! They could have stayed in their pyjamas and got that from the internet. YOU HAVE TO ASK FOR THE SALE. It's your job. You are in a shop. You sell things. Your customer wants to buy things and providing you have done the previous steps properly and with the customer's needs in mind, YOU MUST ASK FOR THE SALE.

So, if this is what we are supposed to do, why don't we do it? Fear. Plain and simple. The original fear you had of approaching the customer and risking rejection transforms itself into the fear of asking the customer to buy your product and them saying no. A good salesperson will overcome this fear and ask the question. A poor salesperson (translated - a cowardly one) will justify why they didn't ask the question. They will come up with no end of excuses why they didn't close the sale. 'The customer wasn't displaying any buying signals'. 'They didn't look like they wanted it.' 'They didn't know what they wanted.'

The list is endless. I know because I have used all of these excuses at some time or another. The truth is, I didn't ask for the sale. I was afraid of rejection.

Here's the secret. Even though you might think you know what the customer is thinking or feeling, you could be, and quite often you may be, completely wrong. You will never know if you don't ask for the sale. Even if you feel like they aren't going to buy, ask anyway. Several times in my career I have been unsure about the customer purchasing. I wasn't getting buying signals. They were playing their cards very close to their chest when I was asking them questions. So I asked them for the sale anyway even though I thought there was no way then were going to buy it. Guess what? They bought it! So even when you think in your own cleverness that they won't buy, ASK FOR THE SALE!

<u>Closing questions</u>
- So, shall I ring that up for you?

- So shall we start on the paperwork?

- Would you like to take that one today?

- How soon would you like this delivered?

- I have one in stock; would you like to take it?

- Will you be paying cash or credit?

- Are you happy with that one?

- Will you take the brown or the blue?

- The best price I can give you is ----, will you take it?

- How would you like to pay for that?

- Shall I see if it is in stock?

- Would you like me to add that up for you?

- So which one will you be taking?

- Would you like that gift wrapped?

- Would you both like some time to decide which way to go? (Used for large purchases, it gives them space but also asks for a decision)

Some people think that closing questions are pushy and that it's pressuring the customer into making a decision. It's not. You are operating under the assumption that the customer has entered your store with the intention of buying something. People don't go into stores to look at things, although they will tell you they are just looking. They go in to see if there is anything interesting enough in there to buy.

Here you are, having spent however long with the customer at the point where you are going to ask them to purchase. You have established rapport, done your homework on what they are looking for, have found them the perfect solution to their query. If you don't ask them to purchase you have done them a disservice. Remember, they have taken the trouble to get dressed, travel to their shopping destination, find a parking space, locate your store, get comfortable with you, describe what they want, looked at all you had to offer and decide which one they like. Why would they go to all that trouble and them not purchase the item?

ASK FOR THE SALE!

TURNING OBJECTIONS INTO OPPORTUNITIES

Many salespeople fall at this last hurdle. They fear it and they feel like all their hard work has been for nothing.

An objection is when you ask the customer if they are ready to make a decision and they come up with a reason to delay the decision. Things like

'I'm not sure.... I need to think about it'

'I don't know ... It's a lot of money'

'I need to see what else is around'

The list could go on and if you are already working in retail you will have your own list of things people say when you ask for the sale.

DON'T PANIC! Objections are a GOOD THING. Seriously, an objection is a buying signal. The fact that they are considering buying it is the best thing that could happen to you. If you get an objection, you know that if you can overcome it you have the sale in the bag. For example, if they are not sure, what are they not sure about? Is there something they need you to go over and explain more fully? Do they need more information on the product? You may need to revisit their needs at this stage to uncover any other functions or purpose for the product. Are they worried that the shoes won't go with their handbag? Are they worried what their Auntie Beryl will say? (You may laugh at that one but to some people, what family thinks is very important). Do you need to help them find a way to pay for it? (i.e. do you need to sell them finance). You need to find out the reason for their indecisiveness and help them get through it.

How to handle some common objections - What to ask.

Before you ask anything at all you must acknowledge their objection. You can't just ignore it and barrel on regardless of their concerns. If you address it directly after acknowledging it, the customer will know that you understand what they are saying and that you are still on their side. Objections are hard for some people to voice also, because they don't want to offend or upset you. After all, you have this great rapport with them. It's like going to a dinner party and you don't like the food. It's hard to say to the host that you can't eat it. This is why some people will make those vague statements and delay making a decision. It's understandable, but hey, if I got upset every time a customer said no to me, I'd be an emotional wreck. We get 'no thanks' all day from people. Think of those dudes that hang around malls and ask people to sign up for charity donations. They get no a hundred times a day and they handle it. The difference is, you have built up a relationship with the customer and they just don't want to offend you so they give you a bunch of guff. Don't worry about it. Just go back in and find out what the real reason for them not saying 'yes' is.

Here are a few you can try -

- Is there anything else you need to know about, or that you are unsure about?

- I can understand you might not want to rush into a decision, but I don't want you to leave without having all the information you need, so is there anything else I can tell you about the product?

- Well, you could come back later on, but I don't want you to be messed around, so is there anything I can do to help you to make a decision so you don't have to make another trip back here?

Other methods of overcoming objections :-

Remind the customer of all the effort they have put in to get to this point. They've done their research, measured what they need to measure, worked out how much they are willing to spend, sought out the store they think they can get the best deal from etc....

Reassure the customer that what they are buying is the right thing for the purpose they described to you. All some people need is a bit of reassurance that what they have in front of them is what they need. If you have built rapport well enough, they will take this direction from you. Say to them 'So it's the colour you want, the size you want, the price you want, and it will do the thing you want it to, we have it in stock and you can take it right now. What do you think? Shall we go for it?"

Okay, so what if they give you that old chestnut 'I'm not sure I can afford it'?

There are a few things you can try that will depend on the type of business you are in.

You may be able to offer payment options if your company has those. You know, pay nothing until next forever, interest free etc. If your company doesn't have these facilities, perhaps let the customer know which credit cards you take. Credit cards are there for the convenience of the customer, that's why they own one!

Explain to the customer how much the item will cost next week, next month or year as appropriate. This will make them think very seriously about how much they will save if they buy it now. Prices go up more often than they go down. This is easy if it's something you have on special.

Remind the customer of how much they need that item, which is why they are there in the first place. You should have uncovered their need for the item at the beginning of the process when questioning them about what they are looking for.

If it's a luxury item, tell the customer they deserve it. I'm sure they work very hard for their money and everyone deserves a treat every now and again. How often your customer chooses to do this is not up to you. I mean, how many pairs of heels or how many handbags does a girl really need?

If you are having trouble overcoming a particular objection, discuss it with your colleagues. Ask them how they deal with it. If they don't know, work on it together and then you can all benefit.

CUSTOMERS WHO ASK FOR DISCOUNT

Unless you own the business, people who ask for a discount can be a bit dreadful. Even if you own the business you probably won't want to give it because every bit of discount you give someone eats away at your profit margin. You may not think it is important that you look after the company profits, but if your store is less profitable than another store, what do you think is going to happen when you ask for a pay rise or a promotion? Even if you are able to discount items, try not to.

There is also the argument that, 'if you don't ask, you don't get' and rightly so. I am hopeless at asking for a discount because of a deeply programmed belief that haggling is only for people in countries where they do haggle and the idiotic notion that if they could sell it for cheaper, they would. I have paid far too much for most things all my life. I understand that this doesn't mean that other people should do the same and I am never offended when people try to haggle with me. However, thanks to a bunch of well-meaning discount-hunting experts and the people who have read their books, some people think that they can get a discount on everything in sight. What most of the discount-hunters are trying to show people is that if you are smart, you will shop around for the best deal. Only a few of them advocate performing a slow, tedious and occasionally excruciatingly tortuous negotiation session with the sales person. These people will make up stories about what they can get elsewhere (if that's so, then what are they doing in your shop?), they will blatantly ask you for money off the price, they will ask you to 'throw in something extra' (they don't usually care what this thing is as long as they think is has some value) and they will threaten to leave if you don't give them what they want. So how do you handle a situation like this?

If your company has some sort of discounting policy, use it to your advantage but do so sparingly. Many companies have 'wriggle room' built into their prices and allow you to use it to close the sale. Don't go into the negotiation with your best offer straight away with these people. Give them a little bit at a time and see what you can do. If this was your business, how much would you give them? If they accept the offer, great!

If your company does not have a discounting policy, explain to the customer that you would like to and if it were your business you would, but you are unable to give them a discount. Then go on to tell them again of all the great features and benefits the product has. If you have done the features and benefits bit brilliantly you will not get the discount question because the customer knows what a great product they are getting. The phrase ' you get what you pay for' springs to mind here. You may also want to add that if they buy from you they will get excellent service from you again if anything goes wrong with the product. After care is very important to the customer especially if it is something that they will be using for an extended period.

WARNING ABOUT WHEN THEY WANT TO CHECK WITH SOMEONE ELSE

If a customer says they need to talk to their husband, wife, boyfriend, girlfriend, mother, father, DO NOT try to tell them that they don't need that person's opinion or that they shouldn't have to talk to them about it before they decide. This will alienate your customer instantly and is quite rude and insulting because it's the same as telling them that they are incapable of making a decision and that they are weak. It is perfectly acceptable for the customer to want to discuss it with someone else, particularly if it is a high-priced item or is something they will have for a long time. The best you can do here is empathise by saying something like, 'Yes, I know. My husband/wife would have something to say if I made a decision like that on my own!'(insert laugh). Your customer will then feel heard by you and recognise that you are on their side. If you say this, they may decide that they can make a decision on their own after all or they may still want to talk it over with someone. The only thing you could do then is to offer your customer the use of a phone to call the person, perhaps send a picture message or give them a brochure and details of the item to take away with them. Anything else will be seen as pushy and will result in a negative customer experience. You need to ensure that the customer will return to buy by continuing the rapport you have built up with them. A colleague of mine, Andrew Blanshard, called this 'be-back dust'. It's a way of describing the things you might say or do to retain the connection with the customer even after they have left the store. You sprinkle a little be-back dust on them as they leave as an expectation that you will see them again soon. It's completely fanciful but I like it! Sometimes it will work and sometimes it won't.

Another one you might try, and this works particularly well for clothing, is to reassure them how well the product suits them and make yourself out to be a shopping guru by telling them this :-

There are 3 rules to shopping,

1. Look at everything

2. Always try it on

3. Don't go home empty-handed because if you do, you've wasted your time.

I have used this one many times and it will often work, if you have created enough rapport and you know the customer wants the item and just needs that nudge to get them to part with their cash. After all, they have come out shopping, they do want to buy something and have probably spent a good amount of time finding the item, trying it on, getting the best fit, so they have invested time and energy into selecting the product and it will be a waste of their time if they did not purchase it.

FINISHING THE SALE

Add-ons - How to multiply your effectiveness

Your company will probably ask you to sell add-ons or accessories to complete the sale. These could be insurance, finance, a belt, fabric protection, extended warranties. Apart from your company's need to make the most of every sale that comes through the door, a higher profit and better return on their investments (you, the store, the product), what is most important is how these products help your customer. It is also a sure-fire way to increase the money in your pocket as most companies offer an incentive to sell add-ons.

For example, insurance on a product will help the customer afford to replace it if it is damaged or stolen. If I had a penny for every customer who had dropped their phone in the toilet and didn't have insurance to replace it, I would have about £60,000 per year. Another £40,000 for those who drop it in a pint of beer or a cup of tea. Not only does the poor customer have no phone to use until they can buy a new one, the new one usually isn't nearly as nice as the one they got free with their contract. It is your job to make sure that the customer understands the benefits to them of purchasing the insurance. They must understand what the warranty covers and what it doesn't. Also you need to let them know how likely it is that their product will suffer from adverse circumstance. For example in the first three months of owning a mobile phone, one in four people will have their phone stolen from them and one in five will accidentally damage it in some way. Once people understand this they are more likely to take the insurance on the phone because they can imagine being one of those people. You must be persistent with this also, after all no-one wants insurance but they sure as heck need it! Most of the time with insurance, extended warranties, fabric protection etc you are selling them peace of mind. If something goes wrong, they don't have to worry about it. The company will sort it out for them.

What if you don't have products in your store that need such things as extended warranties etc? What if you sell relatively disposable items such as clothing? If the customer buys a gorgeous new skirt and then takes it home to find that they have nothing in their wardrobe to go with it, how do you think they would feel? Or if they take it home and the shirt they put with it is a bit long in the tooth the new skirt will make it look even more shabby. There is nothing worse than taking something you have bought home and realising you can't wear it because you have nothing to wear it with! My mother-in-law did this for the outfit she was going to wear to our wedding. She found a beautiful skirt to wear, but the sales assistant didn't show her a top to go with it, or shoes or a jacket. So there she was with a lovely skirt and nothing else. She could hardly come to the wedding in just a skirt! She ended up returning the skirt, shopping at another store, where the salesperson created an entire outfit for her. She looked gorgeous! So, the salesperson in the first shop wasted both their own time and my mother-in-law's and made nothing in the end. The second sales assistant created a lovely outfit, sold her considerably more, which cost considerably more, and her customer went away happy with her purchase. Which sales consultant would you rather be?

I used to do this regularly when I sold mens casual shirts. The fashion was to wear a casual shirt with a t-shirt underneath. I asked my customers if they had a t-shirt to wear under it, to which they would usually reply, yes. I then asked them if the t-shirt they were thinking of was new or old? If it was old, then the new shirt would make the old t-shirt look even older and take away the smartness of their new shirt. Nine times out of ten they would take the new t-shirt which was only a fraction of the price of the new shirt anyway and did not make their final bill significantly higher.

If you are very good, you can build an entire outfit for the customer just by showing them what goes with the item they are interested in. If they are trying on jeans or trousers, grab a belt and put it on them! Just to show them how it will look of course (wink, smile). Get them to try it with shoes, grab a necklace, tie, bag, earrings, anything thing you can think of that will complement the item they are buying. It is very important at this stage to ensure that you have closed the sale on the first item. You need to make sure they are committed to buying it or they may feel overwhelmed at the idea of purchasing the whole lot. They are very likely to take at least one of the items you suggest which will help you reach your targets and get you noticed as a top sales person.

Many shoppers out there don't really know what to wear. They think they have an idea and some of them might actually be able to put it all together successfully, but if you look at people on the street you will realise that most don't have a clue. How often do you see brown belts with black pants and black shoes. Natural tones with brights? It is your job to create an entire look for your customer. If you do, they wear it and get compliments for what they are wearing from their friends, family and colleagues. Where do you think they will go next time they need something new? Where will their friends, family and colleagues go when they need some help getting the look they are trying to achieve right? To you of course!

If you sell furniture and don't sell the fabric protection to go with the new sofa and then the customer's best friend spills red wine on it, the customer has a ruined sofa and may also lose the friendship. (well, only if they are shallow and petty and value inanimate objects more than friendships but at the very least they will regret not getting the fabric protection when it was offered).

In these examples you would be doing a disservice to them if you had not at least offered the product and explained the important advantages of having it added to their purchase. Imagine buying a battery operated toy from a store and then giving it to a child without the batteries. How bad would you feel? If only the salesperson had noticed that it needed batteries and asked you if you needed to buy some of the ones they had conveniently near the counter! It would save a lot of tears.

In the case of extended warranties, it may be helpful to have some general facts or statistics about the likelihood of the product needing to be replaced and in what sort of time frame. For example, I have owned 3 computers in the last 5 years. 2 of them have failed me just after the 1 year warranty has run out. If the salesperson had sold me the extended warranty properly and not just mentioned it as an afterthought I may have saved myself some money.

The main point here is work out why you should sell add-ons, how they benefit the customer and treat this part of the sale as importantly as the original sale you have closed. If the add-on product is vitally important it may help to 'bundle' the cost of it into the price for the customer, with the option of removing it later if they decide to take the risk of not purchasing it.

When selling an add on it is important that you introduce it before you get to the till point. What do we do at the till? We pay and we leave. For example, if I was buying a pair of shoes and the salesperson waited until I got to the till to ask me if I wanted to buy polish, suede protection spray, insoles or grips, I am very likely to say no. I've got what I came for, I'm ready to pay and leave. However, if while I'm trying on the shoes and walking about in them the salesperson describes the material the shoes are made of as patent leather which is strong, durable and incredibly glamorous, but tends to scuff quite easily I would listen. If they then give mea solution to this problem in the form of a product, when I get to the till and they ask me if I would like to take it, I'd be crazy not to! So make sure you present the idea of why they will need the add on product during the sale and not just at the end.

    Bundling the price of add-ons into the total price of the sale is a great technique for getting your customer to take the extras your company provides. When they ask how much something is, include the price of the extra item, which you will of course have introduced before this time, and give them the total package price. Tell them how much and what it includes. You can always adjust the price down if they say no to the add-on. One analogy I use to describe this to my people is, imagine if you were buying a car and seat-belts didn't come as standard. As a good salesperson, you would bundle the price of the seat-belts into the price, right? There is always the opportunity to take them off the price, but why would they? Remember, be persistent if they do say no to it. Reinforce to them how important it is they take the extra service or item and how the product they are buying won't be properly complete without it. In my experience, you can get three no's before you need to back off and leave it.

Chapter 3: DEALING WITH CUSTOMER PROBLEMS

Anyone who has ever worked in retail can tell you stories of 'problem customers' that made their blood boil with their unreasonable expectations, demanding ways and their aggressive attitude and down-right rudeness. Unfortunately in retail we will eventually come across a situation where the customer has a problem with a product or a service. Assuming that you or your colleagues have done a good job with satisfying the customer's needs in the first place, there are techniques you can use to have this disgruntled person leave the store happy and satisfied. Remember, there is no such thing as a 'problem customer', only customers with problems.

Using your empathy skills

Firstly you must listen very carefully without interrupting or getting defensive. Let the customer have their say about what is bothering them. At this point they are always right. I can hear some of you more experienced sales people out there groaning and saying that the customer isn't always right and that 'buyers are liars', but really at this stage you just want the customer to get it off their chest. Let them speak. Nod along, say things like, 'I see, right, mmm, okay' and reiterate to them your understanding of what they are saying, i.e., 'so what you are saying is ....' This tells the customer that you are hearing what they are saying and are empathising with their problem. It also has the effect of taking the emotion out of the situation and bringing the problem back down to it's actual size because you are simply stating the complaint and how the customer feels.Sometimes, if it is a service-related problem, this is all the customer needs. Letting you know they are not happy with the service they received and get their indignation off their chest, knowing they have been heard, is all it takes for them to go away satisfied. You need to imagine what it must be like for the customer to have the problem that they have.

Get into their world, or into their shoes. Another good thing to do is to not put the counter between you and them when having this type of conversation. Go around to the side they are on. This sends a powerful message, that you are on their side.

So listen, empathise and acknowledge their complaint.

<u>Apologizing even if they are wrong.</u>

Second, you need to offer the customer an apology. Yes, that's right -apologise. Even if they are WRONG! The type of apology you give them will depend on the situation and whether the complaint is reasonable. For example, if the customer has received poor service from one of your associates, apologising to them for that experience and then assure them that relevant steps will be taken to correct the error or the incident will be brought to the relevant people's attention. That is probably all they are looking for. If, however, the customer is making unreasonable demands on a product or service and it is more a case of they bought something that did not suit their needs despite being explained the features of the product, you may only be able to offer them an apology like 'I'm sorry you feel that way....' or, 'I can understand your concern.....' These situations are tough ones and you need to be careful not to take the customer's upset personally. You need to put pressure on the system and not on yourself. For example, say I have sold a customer a bed that needed to be ordered. In between placing that order and the warehouse receiving the order, the item has sold out and instead of it taking 2 weeks to arrive in store, it will take 6. I call the customer and let them know about the problem and they become irate and upset at the inconvenience this will cause them. I listen to and acknowledge their concern, apologise for the delay. They are still not happy, but what can you do? Go out the back and start whittling them a new bed? This is when you have to remember to not take it personally and to put the pressure on the system. If the stock-ordering system you have where you work sometimes results in this kind of problem, what can you do about it? Sure, you can complain to your boss or the relevant department, but there is nothing you can do right now. All you can do is tell the customer that it is a problem we sometimes have, in a perfect world it would never happen and that the company is working towards solutions to eliminate the problem. DO NOT go into a great long diatribe about how the system operates and why this problem has occurred or which computer system is inadequate. They do not want to hear any of that, they just want to know what you can do about it. If there is nothing you can do you need to be honest with them. Don't ever make something up to give them false hope about their problem being magically resolved, you will only have a bigger problem and an even more upset customer later. Always under-promise and over-deliver. If the customer is asking you to do something that is physically possible, such as replace an item that you do have in stock, but it would be detrimental to the business if you did and your company asks you not to do this, explain to the customer that you would LIKE to give them a brand new whatsit, but unfortunately you are unable to. You must suggest an alternative solution to the problem. Can the item be repaired? Can it be replaced with a more affordable item? They may not be happy with anything you offer, but at least they will feel that they are back in control because you are giving them options and they are deciding what is acceptable and what is not. This also shows that you are listening, that you are trying to help them and that you care enough to not try to fob them off. It is always better to do this than just say, 'Sorry I can't help you'.

Then you need to find out what it is that would make the customer happy. Often after they have finished venting, and you have summarised their complaint, you can just ask them straight out, "What can I do to make you happy?" Whether you can do what they ask will be up to company policy and procedure. Often it is enough that you reassure them that whatever it is will not happen again. Offer an apology!

What if you have done everything you can to help your customer, empathised, offered solutions and none of it is good enough and they are still all red faced and shouty? If there really is nothing you can do, you may have to accept the fact that either the customer's expectations are too unreasonable or that their issue isn't with you, it's about something else going on in their life. Perhaps there has been a build up to the confrontation they are having with you. You know, you get out of bed, stub your toe, the water heater has blown up, the milk for your tea has gone off, someone cuts you off in traffic, you get a rude text from your mother-in-law, can't find a parking space and then you get top the shop and there is a queue. What are the chances that you will be in a good mood when you discuss your problem with the sales assistant, even if they empathise with you? It's just not fair! I just want something to go right today! I want a win! Do you follow where I am going here? This customer is doing their best to be so confrontational that you will back down. They think if they shout loud enough in front of your other customers that you will back down. Here's the thing, though - never be worried about what the other customers are thinking or how they will react to what is going on. If they see someone losing it at you, they will usually feel sorry for you and that the customer is being an idiot. This customer is not going to be happy unless you give them exactly what they want, and if you can't, things may escalate. If the customer becomes abusive and swears at you, walk away. Just walk away. Especially if you feel yourself getting upset or angry. You must, under no circumstances, ever ever ever be confrontational with them. You are representing your company and it is never acceptable to shout or swear at your customer. Just walk away. If you have asked them to leave and they don't, you are within your rights to have them removed by security or the police. I have had to do this a few times and it is absolutely awful, but the alternative is to be abused by someone. I don't get paid to be abused and the companies I have worked for won't allow me to be abused. It is a very unfortunate situation to be in and I'm glad to say that it doesn't happen often, but the important thing is that you remain in control of yourself. You can't control the customer but you can control your reaction to their behaviour.

Chapter 4: ADVANCED SELLING TECHNIQUES

It's a numbers game

The more customers you approach the more money you will make. If you approach 10 people a day the most you can make are 10 sales. If you approach 50 people a day the most you can make is 50 sales. Which would you prefer? So get out from behind that counter, get out of your office or get away from that other salesperson who chatters to you all day and approach your customers. Remember Matt Staines? He won awards and made loads more commission than everyone else because he would always be the first person a customer saw when they walked through the door. If he didn't greet the customer coming through the door it was because he was already serving one or two or three at a time.

It is worth noting at this point that you need quality as well as quantity. You need to make the most of the customers that come through your door. There will be days when the footfall will be lower than usual and you need to sell more to the customers you have. Also, if you are 'burning' customers i.e doing a poor job of selling to them and they walk without buying anything, your colleagues will soon become ticked off with you. So, don't try to serve everyone at once and do a rubbish job of it, serve as many people as you can give quality service to.

Using social pressure

Another way to reassure the customer that they are making the right decision in purchasing the product is to tell them that the item is very popular, that everybody is getting it, that stock is running out fast etc. This tells the customer that the decision they are making is in line with decisions made by other people. You can only use this if it is TRUE! Do not try this one if it isn't true. The customer will be able to tell as it will come across as insincere and as though you are trying to manipulate them. You must also have a reason why the product is popular, running out fast etc to back up your statement. If it's not true then you will not be able to do this. You need to be careful using this one too. Some people don't want to be like other people, they want to be different from everyone else, so this technique will have the effect of switching them off completely. However, if you have found out the customer's motivation for buying the product you will know if this is the right technique to use or not.

<u>What to say when you get 'Just looking thanks.'</u>

If you are very good, a bit cheeky and very determined, when a customer says, 'just looking, thanks' you will say, 'Okay, what are you looking for?'. When I worked at the furniture store, the area manager was visiting and after I had approached a customer and got "Just looking thanks" I walked back to the manager. He said to me, "Why aren't you serving that customer?" I told him that the customer was just looking. He asked me, 'What were they looking for?' I didn't know the answer. My boss put me on the spot and told me to go and find out what they wanted. At first I was a bit scared of doing this and felt a bit stupid, but nothing terrible happened. The customer just told me what they were after and the sale progressed from there. If I hadn't gone back, they would probably have left without buying. I haven't looked back since. It takes guts to come back and ask a customer what they are looking for when they say they are just looking, but if you don't, you could miss an opportunity to make the sale. Also, from the customer's point of view, you could save them time by getting right to the point and letting them know if they are looking in the right place for what they want, or if they are barking up the wrong tree. As I mentioned before, many of your customers say they are just looking as an automatic reflex to a greeting by the sales person.

So don't be put off, be fearless and seize the opportunity and watch the difference it makes to your income and standing in the company you work for.

Serving multiple customers - how juggling can make you more productive.

Another way to increase your sales volume is serve more than one customer at once. This may be easier in some businesses than others. For example, if you work in a fashion store, you can serve one customer and while they are trying on their items, you can begin to serve another and another and another until you are dashing around the shop floor in a flurry of fabric. If, however, you are selling cars, this represents a greater investment on the customer's part and would therefore require a greater investment of time and attention on your part. Furniture would be somewhere in between. You could leave your customer briefly to discuss the purchase with their partner. Do not, however, leave your customer completely. It may be helpful to imagine that you are joined to them by a fine invisible thread. If you leave them, you just let out a little more thread. This way you will feel the tug on the line when they want your attention or are, horror of horrors, about to leave.

Mirroring - How this technique can get the customer to trust you.

Mirroring is a way to make the customer feel comfortable and at ease with you. Everyone likes people they perceive to be like themselves and if you mirror a person's body language, this will contribute to that feeling. You can also get a person to open up and relax more if they are tense. First you must mirror them for a while and then get them to mirror you. This will happen quite naturally as we are programmed to do this somewhere deep down in our wiring. For example, if you are talking to someone who has their hands in their pockets (classic 'I'm not engaging in this process' body language) you put your hands in your pockets. So you talk to them for a while and get their attention and they may take their hands out of their pocket and cross their arms ('I will listen, but I'm not buying'), so you cross your arms. Then, try doing this. Try as you talk uncrossing your arms to make a point in your speech and then crossing them again a few times and see if they release their arms at all. If they do, you can then get them to adopt a more open posture (wrists exposed) and then you know they are listening to you and trusting what you are saying. Try it out the next time you are having a conversation with someone and see if you can get them to adopt your body language. Have fun with it.

Another great technique I have used often is to nod. If you ask a customer a question, nod your head when you do it if you want them to say yes. If you have begun to mirror each other, the customer will nod with you and it is very difficult to say no when you are nodding your head yes. Some people might say this is manipulative, but if you have your customer's best interests at heart and are showing them what they want or need, then there is no harm in it at all. You are merely getting the customer to communicate their agreement with what you are saying. If they don't agree they will not nod! They are likely to give you a more emphatic no if they really don't agree. This will help you to find out instantly if you are on the right track with what you are proposing.

Another aspect of mirroring is matching the pace of your speech. If your customer speaks slowly, you speak slowly. If they are talking fast, you talk fast. It's a basic thing that most salespeople forget to do.

He who speaks first loses - don't try too hard!

There comes a time in every sale where you should just shut up! When you have given the customer all the information they need to make a decision and asked them to make that decision, in other words you have recapped and closed, you need to wait. Wait! Wait for their response. If you pause and wait and get nothing, you will lose the sale if you speak. Why? The customer has been asked all they can be asked and if you say anything it will sound like you are begging for the sale, which will either make you seem desperate and pushy or will cast a shadow of doubt over the product that you seem so desperate to flog. You will sound desperate. Wait! This will put a small amount of pressure on the customer and force them to make a decision of some sort. Remember you are not pressuring the customer in an uncomfortable way, you are merely giving them the nudge that they need to decide to buy. If there is anymore to be said here, if they need more information, they will ask questions. If they do ask questions, the sale is in the bag. Remember, objections or questions are buying signals. It means the customer wants the product if you can overcome this last hurdle, which you will be able to if you have done your ground work and are recommending the correct item.

There is one very important thing to note here. YOU MUST HAVE ASKED FOR THE SALE BEFORE YOU SHUT UP. If you haven't asked for the sale and go for a silent close, you are leaving your success in the lap of the

Gods. Silent closes do not always work. They will only work if you have had at least 4 or 5 objections and have dealt with all of them successfully, if your customer is nodding vigorously along with you and if you load the silence with masses of intent. Even than it is a risky way to go. It should only be used if you have asked for the sale a couple of times already and don't want to come across as pushy. We all need a nudge now and then to make a decision, but never a shove, so a silent close is your friend in this circumstance.

TROUBLE SHOOTING

What was working, isn't working anymore.

Sometimes we can become very successful using a technique or a 'spiel' that seems to work every time. Then, all of a sudden, it doesn't work anymore. When I was selling furniture one of the add-ons we sold was fabric protection for sofas. I was very successful for about 6 months and then suddenly I wasn't. I couldn't get anyone to buy it, but I was doing exactly what I had done all those times that I had sold it. Then someone said to me, 'You need to change your sales pitch'. What had happened was, I had said the same phrases over and over again for months and it had turned into a robotic, monotone, I'm-bored-with-saying-this monster that wasn't helping me or my customer. So I changed it. Immediately I began working on another way of saying what I had said before and adjusting it according to what the customer had told me when I was qualifying them. I also began introducing it earlier into the sales conversation and 'planting the seed'. I had to think about what I was saying again which had the effect of my sounding more interested in the product and more interested in my customer's needs. Lo and behold I was suddenly selling fabric protection successfully again! So if you're in a rut with your pitch and it's not working anymore, change it! Listen to the way your colleagues are successfully selling it and adapt your pitch to suit your style. There is no need to re-invent the wheel here, a few small changes at the beginning will make you think about what you are saying and get you sounding human again.

Your energy level and how they affect your appeal to the customer

When I walk into a store, I immediately have a feeling about that store. You do too. Everyone does. It's an instant sense of right or wrong. A friend of mine calls it 'feeling the love'. When we shop, we walk around the store and if we are not 'feeling the love', we leave. So what is this mysterious thing that makes us feel comfortable and happy to be there or a bit blah and wanting to leave? Well, here's the secret....... it's YOU!

If you are feeling energised, happy in what you are doing and making the customer feel at home in your store, they will 'feel the love' and will spend more time there looking for what they want. If you make yourself approachable by acknowledging the customer, they will feel comfortable about asking you questions.

So how do we keep our energy levels up and make the store an attractive environment to be in? First, you need to make sure the basics are covered like the appearance of your store and yourself, getting enough sleep and eating properly so that you have that energy level. Second, you need to keep busy and look as though you are ready to engage with the customer. How do you do that? If the store is quiet you need to move about and talk. Clean something, even if it is already clean, tidy something, even if it is already tidy. Talk to each other, laugh and be animated. If I walk past a store and see the salespeople sitting around, leaning on counters looking bored, it makes me want to keep right on walking. I have heard the term many times 'creating theatre'. The shop floor is like a theatre and when you open the doors, you are putting on a show every day. You want to entertain people in your store, not just sell them stuff. This comes back to creating rapport and promoting customer advocacy. The customer should feel like they had a great time in the store when they leave. It's your party, remember. So how do we do this? Comment on what they are wearing. If you overhear a part of a conversation, join in. For example, if you hear a customer say they are going on holidays, ask them where they are off to. Try to connect with them in some way. Use your own personality and personal experience to inject some humanity into the situation. Empathise with them if they are complaining about something in life. Comment on how wonderful something is if they are talking about a great experience. Be interested in what is happening for them. If you are really good at this and there is more than one customer in the store you can get them talking to each other and it all becomes one big party. That's how it should feel, like a celebration. Think about the best party you have ever been to. Was everyone sitting around, not talking and looking bored? Of course they weren't! They were talking to each other, moving around, laughing; their faces had expression and their hands were gesticulating wildly. They were having fun. That's what you need to do to keep energy levels up and create theatre in the store, making it a comfortable environment to be in and get the customer to stay in the store in order for you to make your sale.

The importance of consistency in your performance

So here you are with your toolkit of skills that you've practised and have developed to a high level of performance. What now? Consistency. You have to be consistent in your performance if you want to be successful. You need to practise your skills day in and day out. Sure we all have bad days, but a good salesperson will not allow those days to be many. You are there for 8 hours every day. Make the most of it. Maximise your potential by delivering your strengths every, single day. The company you work for will love this because it will show that you are a safe bet, you are reliable and that what you have achieved isn't just a fluke. People will listen when you speak because you deliver your numbers consistently and therefore must know what you are talking about.

I'm not talking about doing the same thing day in day out. We all need to keep evolving and learning and developing ourselves. I know you want to do that because you are reading this book. What I'm talking about is consistently finding new ways to improve your results, which means constantly working on yourself and working with your colleagues to improve your performance. Every time you hit a target, you will not only be expected by your boss to repeat that success, but also to improve on it! What else would they expect? What would you expect if it were your business? I can think of nothing worse than just plodding along day in and day out doing the same thing and getting the same result. This will not get you noticed or lead to any type of advancement. You need to be consistent in your progression and improvement, so never stop learning, never stop honing your technique and share your skill and knowledge with your peers. You will then be part of a consistently high performing team and will get the associated kudos.

Feedback is a gift (Even if it doesn't feel like it at the time)

If you are serious about getting better at what you do, you need to seek out feedback from the people you work with. You will only get so far by analysing your own performance, you need a different viewpoint if you want to progress further. You will have to ask for it from your colleagues or the people you manage. They will not usually offer it voluntarily as they may not feel they have the right to. However, if you don't ask for this feedback it may come out as a criticism, which is harder to take. Your line manager will give it to you, but if you wait for them to give it, it feels very different than it would if you had asked for it. It is much easier to hear things about yourself that need improving if you have asked for that help, rather than being told that something needs work.

Feedback is a gift, though, because it is an insight into how others perceive you which is not something you can easily do for yourself. It also takes courage and trust to give someone feedback, so you might be grateful that the person giving it to you is brave enough and trusts you enough to do so. It is a sign that your relationship with them is good and that they have your best interests at heart.

Having said all that, sometimes it is hard to hear and can be quite an emotional exchange so you need to have courage and trust also. The courage to hear it and the trust in the other person's intention. Cry if you need to, it will only bring you closer to the person you have allowed your eyes to leak in front of. I absolutely hate crying in front of other people, but nothing bad ever happens. I cry, they empathise, comfort me a little, I get some insight into myself and we move on together with a new improved version of me developing right before our eyes. What is bad about that? Yes, it's a bit scary and, yes, we all avoid it and if it happened every day I think I would become a hermit, but it is still a gift.

Perfect practise makes perfect

Louise Ward was my boss for a couple of years and had had great success as a swimmer when she was younger. She once said that if you practise something over and over you may never improve unless your practice is perfect. Why? If you practise something, but your technique is all wrong, repeating the actions will get you nowhere. You may even find yourself developing bad habits that will get in the way of your success. If, however, you perfect your technique before you practise it over and over, your performance will improve. So work out what works before you practice or you could be wasting a whole lot of time.

How never saying 'no' to a customer will get you more sales.

The great Alister Norwood once told me, never say no to the customer, because they don't want to hear it! Whenever possible avoid using the word 'no' when a customer asks you if you stock an item. If they ask you if you sell Levis you don't have to say 'no you don't', you can say that you 'have something even better'. Customers don't want to hear no. They want to hear yes. Imagine you are a customer and you go into a store and ask for something. The salesperson says they don't have it. How do you feel right now? Awful, right? Fed up? Letting out a bit of a sigh because your search is not over? You need to know what products are most popular in your particular field of retail and if you don't have the product the customer is looking for you need to know what you do have that is similar, or superior in some way and be able to explain why they should buy your product and not the other one.

Okay, so what if you are working in a spoon shop and someone asks for knives? Fair enough, you will not be able to persuade the customer to buy a spoon. The best thing you can do is to direct them to where they can buy the item they need. I hate it when I ask a salesperson for a product and all I get is a flat no. It's infuriating! If you sell spoons, you are quite likely to know where they sell a related product such as knives, so give the customer the information. It is likely that when they are next looking for spoons they will remember the friendly, helpful person who helped them find knives and return to your store rather than some other shop.

How your store is like your toolbox.

The environment you work in has a huge effect on how effective you can be. If your store is untidy, has things that are broken, is dirty or systems that do not work, you need to fix these things if you want to maximise your income. I hate shopping where the store is messy. I recently walked out of a store because the section I was shopping in had stuff all over the floor and I couldn't easily find what I wanted. I will not shop in a store that looks dirty, has handprints on the counter or dust balls on the floor. Your customer will not shop with you if your store looks like this. Do something about it. If something is broken, get it fixed. Do not wait for your store manager to do this for you. They may be busy with other things. Look at it this way. Would a surgeon go into theatre to operate with broken scalpels, and equipment missing? Would a carpenter go to a job without his tools working properly? Of course not! You need to make sure everything is working, too. What do you think customers are thinking if you are scrabbling around under the counter looking for what you need? Get it fixed and get it organised. Waiting for someone else to do it will not get you more money. If you don't know how to get it fixed, ask someone. Ask your manager or ask someone in another store and get it right. You may need to be persistent, you may need to push back if you get a no. You need to persuade someone to repair it, you may need to convince your colleagues to help you keep things clean and tidy, but it will be worth it. It will pay off in more money in your pocket!

Chapter 5: DEVELOPING BEHAVIOURS AND TEAM WORK

You can improve your working environment and therefore increase your income by adopting an attitude of encouragement and working with your colleagues as a team. People say it's a dog-eat-dog world out there and you have to look out for number one, and it is true you do have to take care of your customers, your income and your well-being, but never to the detriment of your co-workers. If you behave negatively towards your co-workers and say things to them to try to 'put them off their game' to make yourself look better and more successful, it will only serve to make you look malicious and nasty. It is far better to foster an environment of encouragement and support in the workplace, where everyone is successful. So how to do this? If one of your colleagues does well at something, a big sale, produces a great display, wins an award, congratulate them and tell them what a great job they have done. Tell them you admire them. Ask them how they did it. If you react positively, instead of putting the person down, saying it was a fluke or they got lucky, you will create feelings of camaraderie and friendship which will benefit you financially in the future. Michael Phillington, who worked in a very male dominated and competitive sales environment used a great explanation of the word team.

Together

Everyone

Achieves

More

Developing positive behaviours in those who work around you takes little more than a thanks or a well done when you see them or hear them do something right. If they clean up something that was looking a bit naff, tell them that that looks better and say thanks for doing that. If they are having a great time with their customer and they are laughing and creating great rapport, comment on it and let them talk about how it was for them. By noticing when people do something well or helpful we acknowledge the part they play in the team and it will be more likely that they will repeat the positive action or behaviour. Everyone wants praise and recognition. Give it to them!

Sales success begins in your mind.

Determination is the key to success. If you go to work thinking that you hope today goes well and that if you are lucky, you might make some sales, you will fail. You need to go in with the attitude that you can make it happen. Today. Right now. You need to believe this wholeheartedly and without any doubt in your mind, that what you set out to achieve will happen because you will make it happen. When you interact with your customers you must hold onto that thought and that the time you spend with them is not a waste for them or for you. You need to constantly look for opportunities to sell what you are offering to your customer. If they say no to what you are offering, that is not the end of the conversation. You need to offer them something else. Persistence is vital. It is tough when your customer rejects what you are proposing, but remember they are not rejecting you, they are rejecting the product. You need to re-evaluate or re-qualify and then go back in with another suggestion. You must be determined to satisfy their needs and to close your sale, otherwise you are wasting your time and energy and theirs also. It's no use just trying.

So what if they don't want anything you have? Well, at the very least you have given them great service, you have shown them something they or someone they know might need in the future and most importantly, you have done your job. Your job is to sell what you have. If you have done absolutely everything you can to sell them what you have, you have done your job.

You must also go into the conversation with the customer with the assumption that they will buy from you, today, right now. They have come into the store with their money in their pocket with the intention of buying. If they didn't have that intention they wouldn't be there. So, take the opportunity to take their money.

Chapter 6: CHANGING YOUR ORGANISATION FROM WITHIN

Where you work and the atmosphere there is very important. If you work in a supportive, efficient and forward-thinking organisation which is united on reaching the same goal, you are much better off than if the atmosphere is disjointed, where it's dog eats dog, and where those around you would rather be somewhere else. If you are part of the latter, the good news is, you can change it. It's wildly optimistic, I know. If everyone who ever read this went on to change the dysfunctional company they worked for into a dynamic, progressive and want-to-work-there organisation the world would be an amazing place. What you need to decide for yourself is how much you are willing to put in to making that happen and whether you want that level of accomplishment. Most of the large companies I have worked for have been pretty good at what they do and I have been have only needed to tweak a few things across the company. I have had one opportunity with a small company where I got to restructure a lot of the way they were doing things to make them more efficient. I implemented information and used methods from working at other companies that vastly improved the way they did business. It was great! I would so love to work for a company that was in a complete mess and use my knowledge and influence to correct all the problems. What an achievement that would be!

So if you have decided that you want to stay with the company that isn't going great at the moment, if you can see the problems as opportunities, what can you do about it?

First you need to go in with open eyes and have a really good look at the way things are done, the company's values and its way of treating its people and communicating with them. If you have previously worked for a great company, you will be able to spot the flaws in the not so great one relatively easily. If you haven't worked for a great company, then you will have to let your own personal values be a sort of radar for spotting those problems. Make a list of what you would like to see change and then get started. If you think that you can't change anything, you won't and if you think you can, you will. Who do you think makes changes in companies and comes up with all the great ideas? Is it just the CEO? Of course not! Anyone can do it. More importantly, if you leave it all up to the head honchos, things may never change. If you don't bring problems to their attention, they may never know they exist. They may go on blindly, scratching their heads trying to work out ways to improve things, wasting their time and money, when you had the answers all along. If you do identify a problem, try to come up with some suggestions for correcting it, or at least a direction in which the upper management may be able to pursue a solution. They do not like it if you just whine about something.

Secondly, start with what you can fix easily in your own immediate environment. Clear out any clutter you find and look for ways to make your working space efficient.

Then get to know your colleagues as best you can. I'm not talking about knowing every intimate detail about their lives, just their likes and dislikes, what they do when they aren't at work, something about their family etc. You need to build rapport with them just as you would a customer. Make them feel valued and special. Look for things about them that you can compliment them on. Once you have your immediate environment running smoothly and the people there are happy to see you and to be there the sales results will follow. Any ideas or suggestions you have will have greater credibility.

Next, you need to look outside your store and examine the company and the way it works. It is like a big machine. Some parts of the machine are essential and are kept working well. Some parts don't work as well and some parts may have very low functionality. If you don't speak up about the pieces of the machine that don't work, how will the company ever grow or become more efficient? You are responsible for your working environment and if something in there is inhibiting you in some way you have to do something about it. Even great companies need this help. It can be so many things, computer systems, the way stock is ordered, information distribution or even your boss. I once had a line manager who was so bad at their job I had to do something about it. This person was such a poor communicator that instead of inspiring me and my colleagues they would have us upset and in some instances in tears. I had two choices, I could do something about it or I could leave. I chose to stay because the company I worked for had fantastic values and some really inspiring leaders who were interested in the development of me and others like me, so I did something about it. I made a formal complaint, with evidence to back up what I was saying through the proper channels. This line manager had had other complaints made against them in the past and my complaint was the final push needed for the company to correct the mistake they had made of hiring someone who wasn't right for the job. After that the atmosphere in the entire section of country that this manager had influence over, changed and we went from being the worst under-performing area to one of the top areas in the country. Why? Well, a combination of reasons led to our success, but initially it was because I did something about it. If I hadn't, who knows how long that area would have suffered and how many other people would have left due to poor treatment? People who suffered under one manager have thrived under the replacement. This is just one example and I'm certainly not advocating that all the problems you may be having at work are your boss's fault! The point I am making is that you are responsible for your working environment and it is up to you to change what isn't working for you.

Chapter 7: SELF ADVANCEMENT

<u>Remarkable employees are productive</u>

Don't ever kid yourself that you are indispensable to your employer. You're not. There are dozens of people out there who can do your job. What you need to concentrate on is making sure that your employer sees the value in keeping you on.

You need to show them that you are well worth the money they pay you by consistently outperforming your colleagues and making lots of money for the company. In return for this you will make more money for yourself if you are working on a commission-based wage or you will be offered a promotion at some time. Sounds like common sense doesn't it? However, you would be surprised at how many people I have come across who just coast through their day doing the bare minimum and manage to keep their jobs. These people never get anywhere, however, and are probably kept on due to the cost of training a new person. In today's highly competitive environment savvy employers are looking for people who will do more for them than just coast through. Performance management procedures are becoming more and more widely used to 'get rid of the deadwood' and rightly so. If you are performing at a high level and your colleagues aren't, it can be very dispiriting and will eventually make you resent the effort you are putting in. So employers are very interested in challenging team members and finding the people out there who are willing to step out of their comfort zones and increase their skills and ability levels. If you are one of those people, your employer will see you as a valuable employee and will do everything in their power to keep you on.

A word of caution, though. If you feel that your employer is asking way too much of you and not looking after you or rewarding you accordingly for your extra effort, you may be being taken advantage of. There are no hard and fast rules for working out if this is the case, so you will have to trust your own judgement. Some clues to go by are that your employer doesn't let you have a break during your working day, will repeatedly ask you to work more than your regular hours without compensating you or appearing very grateful, or will give you a hard time if you are genuinely ill. Follow your instincts and get the advice of someone you can trust. You need to make sure your employer is interested in you balancing your work life and your personal life and that you are doing this also.

Increasing your corporate profile - how to get ahead

If you work for a big company and you want to advance in that company, you need to make a name for yourself. You will need to take every opportunity to get those in the higher echelons to notice you. How do you do that?

First, do your job wholly and completely. Do everything that is asked of you to the letter. Make sure you complete all tasks set you on a daily basis. The type of attention you don't want is the kind where your boss has to remind you to do things. How you do this is up to you. Some people use check lists, some use a diary or notepad, but the outcome must always be that everything is completed promptly. Get organised! If you can get things done before they are due to be completed or if you can do things before you are asked, even better.

Next, you need to think about your job and how you can get things done more efficiently. Try to come up with new ideas that will increase productivity and/or profit for the company. To do this you will need a thorough knowledge of your company's policies, products and procedures. Do your homework. Try these new methods or ideas out in your store and then bring them to the attention of your boss and your colleagues. If they like what you have come up with, the new practices will be cascaded to the rest of the stores in your region with your name on it! If you have a good line manager, they will actively promote your ideas and will help you increase your profile.

Another way to increase your profile is to excel at what you do. If you smash all your sales targets on a consistent basis, this will get you positive attention from the higher echelons every time. Nothing talks like money and the people up the ladder from you will see your figures more often than they will see you. If you consistently excel, this will get their attention and they will come looking for you. However, when you reach your goals, you will need to strive for an even higher level of excellence because what is great this week or month is only good next week or month. Never rest on your laurels, keep reaching higher and higher.

Finally, volunteer for roles outside your job description. If you get the chance to contribute to a special project, or your company is looking for suggestions from people who have your area of expertise, go for it. For example, if your company is bringing out a new product and you have a marketing idea, an implementation idea, or you can come up with a way that that product could be sold by your colleagues, speak up. Who knows, your idea could result in the company making a lot of money. Also, next time the company is looking for input or feedback, your name will come up as one of the people to ask.

Some salespeople think doing these extra things is a waste of their time and energy because they aren't getting paid to do extra. They are the people who will still be in the same place for years and years and really there is nothing wrong with that. If they are happy doing the same thing for years, that's up to them, but if you have got this far into this section I'm guessing you want more from your job and have the drive and ambition to advance yourself. So, take every opportunity that comes your way to get yourself noticed for the right reasons, avoid negative attention and create new opportunities for yourself. You have to give before you get.

A word of warning. As you become more involved with colleagues outside of your job role, be careful not to gossip. Don't allow others to gossip to you either. Nothing will bring a halt to your skyrocketing career faster than back-corridor conversations or criticisms about the personal faults and foibles of your co-workers. Keep it professional at all times and only have positive things to say about others. As my grandmother used to say, 'If you don't have anything nice to say about someone, don't say anything at all.' You should have seen how many people there were at her funeral!

Management - is it for you?

So you want to be a people manager, huh? The good news is that with all the skills you have learned from this book and that you have you practised with your customers, you are now ready to move up the management chain.

Louise Ward once said that she had two ears and one mouth and that she used them in that proportion. She always understood what people were saying to her and always knew exactly what to say in response. You must resist the urge to just wing it and react to what people are telling you. Blurting out the first thing that comes into your head will only get you into trouble. I know this because that's exactly what I did for most of my adult life and I couldn't work out why people would go off me when I thought they liked me just fine. I'm not saying to completely ignore your gut feelings about what people are telling you or to be fake in any way, merely to temper it with a bit of thought and perhaps some questions before you give a response. There is a big difference between responding to a situation and reacting to it. If you can learn this difference you will be like my friend, in control of what she is saying and getting clarity and conciseness into the conversation.

Please don't think that learning all the required administration tasks in your store will get you the job of manager. While this may help your employer to see that you are capable, don't forget that retail is all about money. If you don't hit your sales targets as a salesperson, why would your boss think you would hit the store sales targets as a manager? You must hit and exceed your numbers consistently to be eligible for promotion.

Employers are looking for leadership and accountability in their business managers. By that I mean, are you able to get the 'buy in' of your colleagues when you take on a new product or procedure. Do they listen to what you have to say? Are you role-modelling behaviours that are conducive to the ultimate success of your team? Are you able to simplify complex information? Do you see the success of your store as your responsibility and treat it as if it were your own business?

Make some enquiries and find out if your company has any management-training schemes in place and get yourself skilled up. Read books on coaching, people management, listening skills, communication and anything else you can get your hands on that are relevant to your particular branch of retail.

Chapter 8: WHAT I LOOK FOR WHEN INTERVIEWING A CANDIDATE

<u>How to make the right impression at your interview</u>

There are so many good books out there on how to conduct yourself in an interview it's not funny, but I'll tell you what I look for in a potential candidate.

Apart from the required experience and skill set for the particular position I am interviewing for, there are some other things that are just as important. I have always believed that you can train anyone to do 'the job', but you can't teach a person to have the following –

Are they making a good impression on me? Are they trying to impress me with who they are and what they can bring to my team?

Are they engaging me? Are they animated and telling me things that are interesting?

How much eye contact am I getting? There are cultural differences to consider here of course, some cultures consider it rude to look another person in the eye for an extended period. Also you don't want to appear as though you are trying to stare the interviewer down. A good guide is to give as much as you get. Some people are a bit shy or quiet, which is not great for a salesperson, but is not always a complete inhibitor to hiring. Quietly confident people can make great sales people, as the stereotypical salesperson who is loud and brash is not every customer's cup of tea.

Do they have expression in their voice and on their face or do they speak in a monotone and look bored?

Are they expressing themselves easily or am I having trouble understanding what they are saying?

Is their ambition obvious? By this I mean, do they seem keen to do well in the position they are applying for? Are they money- or goal- oriented? What are their career goals?

Do they want to further themselves, or is this just a job to them? If it is just a job to them it is less likely that they will take the initiative when an opportunity presents itself and will be less likely to seek out new opportunities to learn and grow.

Do they listen, think and then respond? Are they hearing and understanding the questions I am asking, and if they are, are they giving them some thought before answering or just blurting out whatever comes to mind?

Do they believe that they are the best person for the job and that I would be mad not to hire them?

- Do they seem relaxed and confident even though they are in a stressful interview situation?

Are they enthusiastic?

JUST QUIETLY....

A word about your appearance.

Your appearance is very important. You are working in front of the public and therefore you must ensure that you look the best you can. I'm not saying that you have to be a super model, just make the most of what you have. What this means is, if you are clean, well-groomed, well-dressed and well-spoken, you will get a better response from customers and colleagues than if you are scruffy, smelly and look like you haven't slept in a week. So do all the things that you need to. What are they? I'm sure you know already.

Get enough sleep.

Eat healthy food

Exercise

Wash you clothes

Get your hair cut regularly

Have well-kept fingernails

Wear some makeup if you are a woman and shave every day if you are a man.

Make sure you smell nice, but don't overdo it with the perfume or aftershave.

Chapter 9: FINAL WORD

So now you should be ready to increase your income to whatever level you want, doing a job you are already doing or are about to get. You know the basics of how to sell and you have some great tips on how to use advance selling techniques to your advantage. Hopefully, you will also be enjoying retail more, getting more out of your interaction with your customers and they will be getting more out of their interactions with you. You will be helping to build the great reputation of the company you work for and you will be a shining example of what is good customer service and what a great salesperson looks like. You will be primed for promotion and on your way to success. Don't ever stop learning, practising your skills or seeking feedback on your performance. If you do, you will stagnate, get bored and have to move on to seek greener pastures when you are already in a green one. I'm not saying you should never change your job, just that if you do, you operate from a position of strength and move from one great job to an even better one. It is completely up to you to make the most of every situation you are in, which is 'the secret' that this book is all about.

Thank you for reading my book. I hope it has given you something to think about, something to work on and you will become more financially successful after reading it and applying the lessons within. I encourage you to take what you have learned here and share it with your colleagues or anyone else you think may benefit from what I have shared with you on these pages. Thank you and good luck!

www.ingramcontent.com/pod-product-compliance
Lightning Source LLC
Chambersburg PA
CBHW051524170526
45165CB00002B/600